THE GOLDEN YEA...

text: David Sandison, Michael Heatley, Lorna Milne, Ian Welch DISCARDEL

design: Paul Kurzeja

SIENA

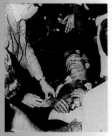

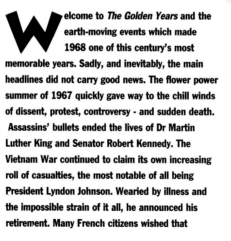

196

Welcome to *The Golden Years* and the earth-moving events which made 1968 one of this century's most memorable years. Sadly, and inevitably, the main headlines did not carry good news. The flower power summer of 1967 quickly gave way to the chill winds of dissent, protest, controversy - and sudden death. Assassins' bullets ended the lives of Dr Martin Luther King and Senator Robert Kennedy. The Vietnam War continued to claim its own increasing roll of casualties, the most notable of all being President Lyndon Johnson. Wearied by illness and the impossible strain of it all, he announced his retirement. Many French citizens wished that

President de Gaulle had done the same in December 1965 as his always autocratic manner gave way to a near-dictatorial approach to unions and students groups, and France dissolved into strikes, riots and a state of near anarchy.

The people of Czechoslovakia enjoyed a few brief months of the relative freedom brought them by the new government of the liberal communist leader, Alexander Dubček. Unfortunately, the communist regime in Moscow was not inclined to liberalism or freedom, and Soviet Army tanks rolled in to end the 'Prague Spring' and Czech dreams of a more open society. Unbelievably, there were tanks in the streets of Chicago too before the year's end when an anti-war

8

demonstration, held to coincide with the Democratic Party's convention to find a successor to President Johnson was brutally smashed by police and troops. Vice-President Hubert Humphrey was the Democrats' choice, but the American people voted for Richard Milhous Nixon.

In Mexico, the cream of the world's athletes pitched themselves in more worthy battles, with records tumbling in the relatively rarefied air 7,000 ft above sea level, and Dick Fosbury proving that you could jump higher than anyone else by throwing yourself backwards over that bar high above the ground.

It wasn't any stranger than some of the things we got up to in 1968!

3

Moderate Dubček to Lead Czechs

THE MODERATE SLOVAK politician, Alexander Dubček, today won what was described as a bitter struggle to emerge as the new leader of the Czechoslovak Communist Party - the first Slovakian to rise to that office and so become effective head of state.

A party official since World War II, when he was an underground fighter, Dubček successfully ousted hardliner and Moscow favourite Antonin Novotny to signal a move towards a relaxation of state control and the beginning of long-overdue economic reforms.

The 46 year old Dubček was well regarded within the party and popular with the people, and was expected to work towards social democracy via liberal reforms. In an indication of Dubček's liberal style, Novotny was praised for his past leadership and made President of Czechoslovakia.

1: Hello Goodbye
- The Beatles
2: Magical Mystery Tour EP
- The Beatles
3: The Ballad Of Bonnie And Clyde
- Georgie Fame
4: Walk Away Renee
- The Four Tops
5: Daydream Believer
- The Monkees
6: I'm Comin' Home
- Tom Jones
7: Thank U Very Much
- Scaffold
8: Everlasting Love
- Love Affair
9: If The Whole World Stopped Loving
- Val Doonican
10: World
- The Bee Gees

JANUARY 20

Hollywood's Dream Couple Wed

Polish-born film director Roman Polanski today married American actress Sharon Tate (pictured), ten years his junior. She'd starred in three successes in 1967, namely *Eye Of The Devil, The Fearless Vampire Killers* and, most notably, *Valley Of The Dolls*, and was very much in the ascendancy as one of the up-and-coming leading ladies. Polanski had directed *Vampire Killers*, and his 1968 release, *Rosemary's Baby*, would establish him as one of the film world's hottest properties.

It seemed a marriage made in Hollywood heaven - but all would go tragically wrong in August 1969 when the pregnant Sharon Tate and four of her friends would be horribly murdered by members of Charles Manson's notorious 'Family'. Polanski, who would hit the headlines in 1977 after his alleged involvement with a 13 year old girl, would be forced to continue his directing career outside the US to avoid arrest.

JANUARY 1

C Day Lewis Is New Poet Laureate

The Irish poet, critic and novelist Cecil Day Lewis today became Britain's new Poet Laureate, succeeding John Masefield who died last year. Lewis, 63, made his name in the 1920s when he had strong left-wing sympathies, although he renounced his membership of the Communist Party in 1939. His alter ego, Nicholas Blake, created over 20 detective novels which were to provide his main source of income and, later in life, Lewis (not to be confused with CS Lewis) became Professor of Poetry at both Oxford and Harvard universities. His son, Daniel Day Lewis, was born in 1957 and would make an early name for himself as a film star in 1971's *Sunday Bloody Sunday* before achieving international acclaim, and an Oscar as Best Actor, playing the multi-handicapped Christy Brown, in *My Left Foot*.

JANUARY 31

Mauritius Granted Freedom

The tiny Indian Ocean island federation of Mauritius today gained its independence from Britain after 158 years of colonial rule and several days of race riots. The country – which is made up of many small islands together with the dependencies of the Rodriques Islands, Cargados Carajos shoals and Agalega – was to be ruled by a coalition government composed of the Muslims, Indians and French Creoles who lived there, although it would remain a part of the British Commonwealth.

ARRIVALS
Born this month:
14: LL Cool J, US rapper
31: John Collins, Scotland
international football player

JANUARY 15

North Korea Seizes US Spy Ship

THE US NAVY SHIP *Pueblo* was today at the centre of an international incident when North Koreans boarded the vessel, taking the crew captive after killing one and wounding a number of others in an exchange of gunfire.

The *Pueblo* - a converted freighter laden with electronic surveillance equipment, but few arms - was sailing in international waters 25 miles off the coast of North Korea when she was captured. Early indications suggested that when the North Koreans first challenged her, two hours earlier, she may have been within the 12-mile national limit.

Four US crewmen were wounded in the incident and all 83, together with the vessel, were impounded at the port of Wonson. So far the Koreans had rejected US demands for the safe return of the ship and her crew. In fact, it would be eleven months before the men returned home, subsequently claiming that they had been tortured and forced to sign false statements.

JANUARY 31

Vietcong Launch Tet Offensive

Communist Vietcong guerrilla forces launched a large-scale attack today, in which no part of South Vietnam was left unaffected. A simultaneous assault on more than 100 cities and towns was timed to perfection, using the Vietnamese New Year, or Tet, celebrations to give an element of surprise to their very effective offensive, even penetrating the US Embassy in Saigon.

The North Vietnamese enjoyed a strong measure of support from many sympathetic southerners, even in the capital city Saigon where the South Vietnamese Army had recently been put in sole control of security. Dressed in South Vietnamese uniforms, Vietcong troops invaded and held the US Embassy for six hours before US forces flown onto the roof by helicopter involved them in a bloody gun battle.

Thirty aircraft were destroyed on the ground at the US airbase at Da Nang, and the guerrillas very nearly succeeded in gaining control of a Saigon radio station.

The Hills Are Still Alive

The soundtrack album from *The Sound Of Music*, Julie Andrews' blockbuster movie (pictured) featuring the music of Rodgers and Hammerstein, hit the top of the UK charts LP today for the 11th separate time. Released in 1965 to coincide with the film, it would spend a remarkable 381 weeks on the UK chart and 161 weeks in the US, peaking at No 1 on both sides of the Atlantic. *The Sound Of Music* won Academy Awards for Best Picture, direction, editing, sound recording and photography. Yet, as the album's success proved, the film's enduring appeal was based on catchy songs like *Do-Re-Mi*, *My Favourite Things* and *Climb Every Mountain*.

FEB

Hue Recaptured As US Viewers Witness Brutal Execution

AMERICAN AND SOUTH Vietnamese forces today celebrated their recapture of the former imperial city of Hue, which had been in the hands of the Vietcong and North Vietnamese Army forces for more than three weeks following the Tet offensive. The ferocity of the fighting, both during the original offensive and in South Vietnam's retaliatory action, shocked an American public who were shown scenes of startling brutality in TV news broadcasts.

The televized event which caused greatest outrage, however, was the summary execution of a South Vietnamese prisoner suspected of communist sympathies. Paraded for the world's TV and print journalists in Saigon, his hands tied behind his back, the man was despatched with a single bullet fired into his head at close range by South Vietnam's General Loan, who told journalists calmly, 'Buddha will understand'.

But while US citizens were losing the stomach for fighting the war, President Johnson was increasing the US commitment by sending in another 10,500 combat troops and cancelling virtually all exemptions from the draft for graduate students. He may have believed that the US had done as much as possible to further the cause of peace, but many of his people believed that too much had been done to no real purpose.

FEBRUARY 1

Presley Heiress Born

The King today produced a Princess – or, rather, his wife did - when a daughter to be named Lisa Marie (pictured), was born to Elvis and Priscilla Presley at 5.01 pm at the Baptist Memorial Hospital, Memphis, Tennessee.

Her birth was to start a spectacular year for Elvis, which would end in December with a TV special, simply entitled *Elvis*, that drew rave reviews and had the year's largest US viewing figures for a musical special.

He doted on his daughter, naming his private airliner after her, but would become legally separated from her mother in 1972. Lisa Marie, meanwhile, grew up to marry Michael Jackson in 1994 after a long period of drug dependency and one other ill-fated marriage.

FEBRUARY 20

Free Milk Ends For Over-11s

There was good news and bad news for the British welfare state today. The House of Commons passed a bill to raise contributions for National Insurance, but at the same time free school milk for children of secondary school age was discontinued, despite the abstentions of 46 rebel Labour MPs.

When, several years later, the Secretary of state for Education, Margaret Thatcher announced that the Conservative Government was cutting free milk for eight to eleven year olds, she was branded 'the most unpopular woman in Britain' by the Sun newspaper and earned herself the name of 'Thatcher, the milk snatcher'.

FEBRUARY 19

Watch Out! There's A Thief About

Rising crime rates, especially thefts, prompted the British Home Office to launch a new anti-crime campaign today, to increase public awareness of the problem.

Launched with the catch-phrase 'Watch Out! There's a Thief About', the police hoped the campaign would encourage people to lock up their valuables against opportunist criminals.

This year seems to have been a year for slogans. In January, five typists from the South London suburb of Surbiton announced that they would work extra hours without pay to boost their small part of British industry - declaring that they were 'backing Britain'. The Government had now picked up on the idea and were planning a poster campaign using the Union Jack with the caption 'I'm Backing Britain'.

UK TOP 10 SINGLES

1: Everlasting Love
- Love Affair

2: The Mighty Quinn
- Manfred Mann

3: Am I That Easy To Forget
- Engelbert Humperdinck

4: Bend Me Shape Me
- Amen Corner

5: Judy In Disguise (With Glasses)
- John Fred & His Playboy Band

6: She Wears My Ring
- Solomon King

7: Suddenly You Love Me
- The Tremeloes

8: Gimme Little Sign
- Brenton Wood

9: The Ballad Of Bonnie And Clyde
- Georgie Fame

10: Pictures Of Matchstick Men
- Status Quo

Born this month:

7: Brian Deane, English football player

12: Chynna Phillips, US pop singer (Wilson Phillips)

14: Molly Ringwald, US actress (*Pretty In Pink*, etc)

26: Geoff Aunger, Canadian international football player

DEPARTURES

Died this month:

13: Mae Marsh, US film actress, silent era star (*The Birth Of A Nation, Jane Eyre*, etc), aged 73

16: Little Walter (Walter Jacobs), US blues harmonica player, singer (long-time associate of Muddy Waters), aged 37

17: Sir Donald Wolfit, UK actor-manager (inspiration for 'Sir' in Ronald Harwood's *The Dresser*), aged 65

20: Anthony Asquith, UK film director (*French Without Tears, The Winslow Boy, The Browning Version, The Importance Of Being Earnest*, etc), aged 65

22: Peter Arno, US cartoonist, aged 64

FEBRUARY 17

Three-Gold Killy Conquers Winter Olympics

Not even the unashamed patriotic chauvinism of President Charles de Gaulle, who performed the opening ceremony of the 19th Winter Olympics in front of an audience of 60,000 spectators on February 6, anticipated the triple gold medal triumph which French skier Jean-Claude Killy (pictured) gave his country today.

The Games, which were being held in the Alpine town of Grenoble, saw all three major men's skiing events won by the customs officer the French referred to as 'le Superman' - the first such 'triple' win since Toni Sailer of Austria in 1956. Killy won the giant slalom and the downhill outright and narrowly beat Austrian Karl Schranz in today's final slalom. Although Schranz had a faster time, he was disqualified after a two-hour inquiry for missing one of the gates.

Immigrants Subject To New UK Law

ASIAN IMMIGRANTS leaving the former British colony in Kenya, which achieved independence six years ago, were causing increasing headaches in the Home Office. While their passports entitled them to enter Britain, many feared that the large numbers entering the country would place undue strain on the local job market - and this prompted the Government to introduce emergency legislation today.

The Commonwealth Immigrants Bill, which was due to get the royal assent early next month, would restrict the number of 'work vouchers' available under the new system to 1,500 per year. At present, almost that many were entering Britain every week.

Last year, the number of Commonwealth immigrants entering Britain increased by more than 20 per cent. The Home Secretary, James Callaghan said 'We have a responsibility to our own people at home, as well as to a million holders of British passports abroad'.

The Beatles Travel To India

George and Patti Harrison, along with John and Cynthia Lennon, travelled to the banks of the River Ganges today, seeking 'absolute bliss consciousness' with their guru, the Maharishi Mahesh Yogi. Ringo and Maureen Starr, Paul McCartney and girlfriend Jane Asher, actress Mia Farrow and singer Donovan would join them three days later.

But harmony proved short-lived - the Starrs would return to Britain before the allotted fortnight was over, reportedly complaining about the 'spicy food'. In June, The Beatles would renounce the Maharishi as 'a public mistake' at a New York press conference. He was also the subject of the satirical *Sexy Sadie* which appeared on the The Beatles' *White* album.

End Of Line For Tragic Teenager

Frankie Lymon, a world star at the age of 13 as lead singer with US doo-wop sensations The Teenagers, was this morning found dead on the floor of his grandmother's bathroom in New York. He was just 25. A syringe was found nearby, and a heroin overdose later confirmed. Lymon died penniless, despite a string of hits including *Why Do Fools Fall In Love* and *I'm Not A Juvenile Delinquent*. His career collapsed after he was persuaded to split from the group, and though he admitted smoking pot at school and sleeping with women twice his age, he was neither content nor financially comfortable. At the time of his death he was attempting a comeback while simultaneously serving with the US Army.

Violent Vietnam Protest At US Embassy

LONDON GOT A TASTE of the atmosphere which had been pervading many US cities in the past few months when demonstrators attacked the American Embassy in Grosvenor Square today. It was the most violent encounter the city had experienced for a number of years.

Several hundred people were arrested when what began as a relatively good humoured rally in Trafalgar Square - where close on 90,000 listened to speeches from actress Vanessa Redgrave, among others - became an all-out battle when demonstrators tried to storm the Embassy about a mile away (pictured).

Mounted police were brought in to try to control the crowd, who used banner poles to attack officers, 90 of whom were injured. Paint and stones were hurled at the Embassy building at the height of the demonstration, and a nearby hotel was also vandalized.

First Man In Space Dies

Soviet cosmonaut Yuri Gagarin, who in April 1961 became the first man in space, died today when a MiG-15 jet trainer he was flying crashed near Moscow.

The son of a humble collective farm carpenter, Gagarin's 90-minute orbit in 1961, during which he travelled at speeds of over 17,000 mph, put the Soviet Union's space programme firmly in the world spotlight and earned him wide acclaim at home.

Since then, the 34 year old had become a sought-after spokesman for the space programme, lecturing all over the world and charming audiences wherever he went. His death was mourned on both sides of the Iron Curtain, and his burial, in the Kremlin Wall, became a national event.

Globe-Girdling 'Galaxy' Unveiled

US aircraft manufacturers Lockheed today showed their latest military transport plane, the huge *Galaxy*, to the world as President Johnson watched the first example come off the production line.

The makers of the workhorse transporter *Hercules* had already produced an impressive jet transporter in the *Starlifter*, but the C-5A *Galaxy* - which would make its maiden flight in June - could carry massive loads, like two M60 battle tanks or a dozen small helicopters, with a 'roll on, roll off' capability achieved by large doors at front and rear.

The *Galaxy* was intended for rapid support of US forces in Europe, should a confrontation situation develop in Germany, and would become the backbone of US Military Airlift Command.

Graham's Fillmore Crosses Continent

American rock music promoter Bill Graham today opened the Fillmore East in an abandoned cinema on New York's Second Avenue, thus providing an east coast counterpart to his legendary San Francisco venue, The Fillmore Auditorium. Tim Buckley and Janis Joplin's Big Brother and the Holding Company played the opening night.

Graham, born Wolfgang Grajanka in Germany, would re-site his San Francisco operation in July to the Carousel Ballroom, renaming it the Fillmore West. Though his venues eventually closed, Graham remained an important and influential figure in US rock - including organizing the US leg of Live Aid - until his death in a helicopter accident in 1991.

UK TOP 10 SINGLES

1: Cinderella Rockefella
- Esther and Abi Ofarim

2: Legend Of Xanadu
- Dave Dee, Dozy, Beaky, Mick & Tich

3: Fire Brigade
- The Move

4: Rosie
- Don Partridge

5: Jennifer Juniper
- Donovan

6: Delilah
- Tom Jones

7: The Mighty Quinn
- Manfred Mann

8: (Sittin' On) The Dock Of The Bay
- Otis Redding

9: Green Tambourine
- The Lemon Pipers

10: She Wears My Ring
- Solomon King

Born this month:
4: Patsy Kensit, UK pop singer (Eighth Wonder) and actress
10: Pavel Srnicek, Czech international football player
15: Sabrina Salerno, Italian pop star
20: Paul Merson, England international football player
23: Damon Albarn, UK pop singer, songwriter (Blur)

DEPARTURES

Died this month:
27: Yuri Gagarin, Soviet cosmonaut, first man in space *(see main story)*

MARCH 15

Brown Resigns From Foreign Office

Britain's foreign friends could be forgiven for being slightly perplexed by the change in style of the UK's Foreign Secretary. Flamboyant George Brown (pictured with his wife), who resigned his post suddenly and unexpectedly today, was replaced by the steady, even staid, Michael Stewart who had held a variety of ministerial jobs during 20 years of political life.

The outgoing minister accused Prime Minister Harold Wilson of not consulting him and of running the cabinet as a dictatorship. But Brown, the son of a London lorry driver, was himself no stranger to controversy and was known to get both tired and emotional when he'd had a few drinks - something he was increasingly prone to do.

MARCH 16

Tragic Otis Hits The Top

American soul star Otis Redding, who died on 10 December 1967 along with four band members when the plane in which they were travelling crashed, reached No 1 in the *Billboard* pop charts today with his *(Sittin' On) The Dock Of The Bay*. Recorded three days before his demise, the song became Redding's first pop and R&B chart-topper. It would also win two Grammies, be covered by Redding's sons Dexter and Otis III, while white soul stylist Michael Bolton would record what Redding's widow would say was her favourite cover version, in 1988.

Robert Kennedy Enters Race For White House

To no-one's real surprise, Robert Kennedy - the younger brother of the assassinated President John F Kennedy - today declared that he was to be a contender for the Democratic Party's nomination in this Presidential election.

A graduate of Harvard University and Virginia Law School, Kennedy's initial political experience was gained during his brother's campaign for election to Congress and, later, when he ran the nationwide network of offices to help him win the Presidency.

Robert Kennedy served as Attorney-General during JFK's administration, and was elected to the Senate in 1964 - a strong advocate for social change in America and now a strong opponent of the US war in Vietnam.

LBJ Decides To Stand Down

DESPITE HIS RECENT WIN in the New Hampshire Democratic Party primary, President Johnson today announced that he would not be seeking re-election to the White House later this year. In the past fortnight he had faced strong opposition to his policies on the conduct of the Vietnam War from within his own party - most especially from his front-line opponents, Senators Eugene McCarthy and Robert Kennedy, who'd announced his candidacy only days earlier.

The President's announcement came at the end of a networked speech and took journalists - who'd had no warning that he'd add words to the text they'd been given in advance - by complete surprise. 'I shall not seek, and I will not accept, the nomination of my party for President', Johnson said, his expression reflecting the seriousness of his words.

With only a quarter of the US public reportedly supporting his foreign policy, LBJ had obviously decided to call it a day. Robert Kennedy recently attacked the President for his 'disastrous, divisive policies' on Vietnam – and although he and Senator McCarthy were proving popular contenders for the Democratic nomination, it was thought that Johnson would urge his Vice-President Hubert Humphrey to join the race.

MAR

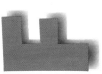

HEPBURN AND STREISAND TIE MAKES OSCARS HISTORY

A moment of sheer theatricality stopped this year's Academy Awards show dead in its tracks when Ingrid Bergman - given the task of announcing the Best Actress award - opened the gilt-edged envelope, did a classic double-take and announced that, for the first time in the Oscars' 37-year history, a major prize had been tied. The title was to be shared by screen veteran Katharine Hepburn and movie débutante Barbra Streisand.

No-one argued with the justice of the decision, even though Americans hate a tie. Although she had won her second Oscar only the year before (for *Guess Who's Coming To Dinner?*), Hepburn's astounding, powerful and moving portrayal of Queen Eleanor in *The Lion In Winter* would probably have given her a third in any other year. But Streisand had made *Funny Girl*, and made the character of Fanny Brice her own with an accomplished début well worthy of peer acclaim.

Hepburn's co-star in *The Lion In Winter* (a film justly in the running for Best Picture, with director Anthony Harvey, writer James Goldman and composer John Barry rightly nominated in their respective categories),

was Peter O'Toole. Like Hepburn, he'd delivered a faultless performance to help create a timeless classic, and could normally have expected a stroll up to make his acceptance speech as Best Actor. Unfortunately for him, Cliff Robertson had made the prize his with a moving portrayal of a mentally handicapped man in *Charly*, so beating O'Toole, Alan Arkin (*The Heart Is A Lonely Hunter*), Alan Bates (*The Fixer*) and Ron Moody's Fagin in *Oliver!*

The last-named film's Oscar for Best Picture, and Carol Reed's victory as Best Director, took many by surprise, not least because Reed had failed to win awards for far better films (*The Third Man*, *The Fallen Idol* and *Outcast Of The Islands*) in the past. Many thought Stanley Kubrick should have won for *2001: A Space Odyssey*. In the event, he did walk off with the Best Visual Effects Oscar as consolation.

No consolation (or major nominations) for *The Thomas Crown Affair*, although Michel Legrand did win an Oscar for his song *The Windmills Of Your Mind*. Vanessa Redgrave (*Isadora*), Joanne Woodward (*Rachel, Rachel*) and Patricia Neal (*The Subject Was Roses*) had to

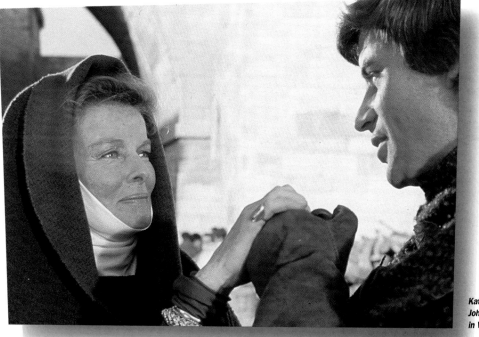

Katherine Hepburn and John Castle in 'The Lion in Winter'

settle for Best Actress nominations on their biographies, though Ruth Gordon's Supporting Actress award for *Rosemary's Baby* was warmly applauded.

William Goldman did win the Adapted Screenplay for *The Lion In Winter*, while John Barry's score was adjudged good enough to give him a matching pair with the Oscar he'd won two years earlier for *Born Free*. The Original Screenplay prize went to Mel Brooks for *The Producers*, while the Best Picture-nominated *Romeo and Juliet* failed to give director Franco Zeffirelli a prize, and only produced one Oscar - for Danilo Donati's costumes.

APRIL

Martin Luther King Killed By Gunman

CIVIL RIGHTS CHAMPION and Nobel Peace Prize laureate, the Rev Dr Martin Luther King Jr, died today in hospital after being shot by a high-powered rifle at the motel where he was staying in Memphis Tennessee. He was only 39 years old.

Dr King, who was born in Atlanta, Georgia, into a strongly religious Baptist family, became involved in civil rights issues in the mid-1950s, modelling his non-violent movement on that of the Indian leader, Mahatma Gandhi, and achieving international fame and support in 1963 when he led a march of 250,000 to Washington DC.

It was on that occasion that he delivered his famous 'I have a dream' speech and the following year he was awarded the Nobel Peace Prize. He was also outspoken against US involvement in the Vietnam War, claiming that resources would be better used fighting poverty at home. Dr King was visiting Memphis to support striking sanitation workers and his death was the cue for rioting in a number of major US cities - including the heart of Washington - despite calls by his widow, Mrs Coretta King, for peace.

Among those gathered to pay tribute to Dr King at his funeral in Atlanta on April 9 (pictured), were Mrs Jacqueline Kennedy, widow of the assassinated president, and Vice-President Hubert Humphrey. The eulogy was delivered by Dr King himself - via a tape recording of his last sermon. Anticipating the likelihood of his own death the night before he was killed, he said, 'Longevity has its place. But I'm not concerned about that right now. I want to do God's will, and he's allowed me to go up to the mountain, and I've looked over and I've seen the Promised Land'.

On April 19 the FBI announced they were seeking a man they named as James Earl Ray, alias Eric Galt, for Dr King's murder. America's black and poor, however, were looking in vain for a new leader.

Muted Congrats As Cliff Comes Second

Britain's Peter Pan of Pop, Cliff Richard, failed to make the most of home advantage at this year's Eurovision Song Contest - staged at London's Royal Albert Hall tonight and presented by the evergreen Katie Boyle - as an estimated 10 million British households tuned in to watch a Cliff-hanger which ended in Cliff's *Congratulations* being edged into second place by Spain's Massiel with *La, La, La.* Later in the month Cliff would make his TV drama début as a 'suave young villain' named Riley in *A Matter Of Diamonds.* 'The character is nothing like me', the squeaky-clean singer insisted, 'and that gives a performer plenty to work at'.

F1 Champion Clark Dies During Race

Scotsman Jim Clark, the Formula One racing driver whose competitive career put Lotus cars on the racing map, died while practising for a Formula Two race in Hockenheim, West Germany, today. Widely acclaimed as the most successful racing driver of his generation, having won the World Championship twice, Clark was on course for a third title at the time of his death. Over the last seven years he had averaged more than three wins per season, in 25 Grand Prix events - which put him ahead of the previous record-holder, Argentinian Juan Fangio, who had retired ten years earlier.

Trudeau Is New Canadian PM

Pierre Trudeau succeeded Canada's outgoing Prime Minister, Lester Pearson, today when he became leader of the Liberal Party and the fifteenth Prime Minister in Canada's history. But he also inherited a small parliamentary majority which prompted rumours that he would be forced to call a general election.

Trudeau was very much a man of the 1960s, having worked as a civil rights lawyer before embarking on a career in politics.

The retirement of 71 year old Pearson meant that Canada lost a senior statesman. He was the first Canadian to be awarded the Nobel Peace Prize - for his mediation in the Suez Crisis of 1956 - and would be immortalized when Toronto's international airport was named in his honour.

UK TOP 10 SINGLES

1: Congratulations
- Cliff Richard
2: What A Wonderful World
- Louis Armstrong
3: Delilah
- Tom Jones
4: If I Only Had Time
- John Rowles
5: (Sittin' On) The Dock Of The Bay
- Otis Redding
6: Lady Madonna
- The Beatles
7: Simon Says
- The 1910 Fruitgum Company
8: Step Inside Love
- Cilla Black
9: If I Were A Carpenter
- The Four Tops
10: Jennifer Eccles
- The Hollies

ARRIVALS

Born this month:

28: Howard Donald, UK pop star (Take That)

29: Carnie Wilson, US pop singer (Wilson Phillips)

DEPARTURES

Died this month:

1: Lev Landau (Lev Davidovitch), Soviet theoretical physicist, Nobel Prize winner 1962, aged 60

4: The Rev Dr Martin Luther King, US civil rights leader *(see main story)*

7: Jim Clark, Scottish Grand Prix driver, former world champion *(see main story)*

16: Edna Ferber, US novelist (*Giant, Ice Palace*), screenwriter (*Showboat, Cimarron, Dinner At Eight,* etc), aged 80;

Fay Bainter, US Academy Award-winning film actress (*Jezebel, Quality Street, The Human Comedy, State Fair, The Secret Life Of Walter Mitty,* etc), aged 76

APRIL 15

Dutschke Shooting Sparks Riots

The attempted assassination of radical West German student leader Rudi Dutschke, by a man claiming to be emulating the killing of Martin Luther King, sparked off a wave of student riots in Europe today.

In Germany, the headquarters of the right-wing Axel Springer newspaper group - said to have created a climate of intolerance - were attacked, while the company's offices in Holland, Italy and Britain were also targeted by demonstrators.

APRIL 27

Powell Delivers 'Rivers Of Blood' Speech

OUTRAGE GREETED a speech by British politician Enoch Powell in Birmingham tonight in which he said, 'As I look ahead I am filled with foreboding. Like the Roman, I see the River Tiber foaming with much blood'.

He was referring to the British Government's policy on immigration – specifically black immigration – which allowed 50,000 Commonwealth citizens and their dependants into Britain every year.

Although Powell believed he spoke responsibly, and vehemently denied whipping up racial prejudice, Edward Heath - leader of the Opposition and Powell's Conservative Party chief - disagreed with his comments just as vehemently, and was likely to sack Powell from his shadow cabinet post. Perhaps what created the most unease was that he merely voiced the fears of many British citizens worried about jobs and pressure on the Welfare State.

APRIL 23

Decimalization Of Britain's Currency Begins

The first step in the gradual process of decimalizing Britain's currency to bring it in line with most world systems began today when the new 5p and 10p pieces – which were identical in size and value to the old one and two shilling pieces – were put in circulation. Next month would see the introduction of a completely new coin when the seven-sided 50p replaced the old ten shilling note.

It already seemed as if the consumer was getting less for his or her money. Although the 'new pence' were, in theory, worth no more than the old 'pennies' (except you had to work out that there were five of them to the old shilling, which was going to vanish anyway, instead of 12 old pennies), it was difficult not to feel hard done by. There was also the often-justified suspicion that some shops were 'rounding up' new money that didn't need rounding up at all.

APRIL 10

Oscars In Space?

While the natural focus in this year's Academy Awards was on Rod Steiger and Katharine Hepburn's Oscars for their performances in *In The Heat Of The Night* and *Guess Who's Coming To Dinner* respectively, all the after-show talk centred on the imminent release of Stanley Kubrick's *2001: A Space Odyssey* (pictured), his adaptation of co-writer Arthur C Clarke's science-fiction epic.

Filmed in England because director and writer didn't want details of the plot to spread, its special effects would set the standard for the pre-Star Wars era, while the revolutionary but little-understood 70mm-Cinerama process in which it was filmed was also a talking point.

Three years and $10.5 million in the making, 2001 was clearly set to stun.

MAY 9

Spring In Prague, But Soviets Mass On Border

SPRING CAME EARLY this year in the Eastern Bloc country of Czechoslovakia, and was staying late. There was real hope among the Czech people, as they watched Alexander Dubček's government relax its hold on the country's political and social life in an effort to achieve its stated aim of 'socialism with a human face'.

The media was freed of strict censorship imposed since the end of World War II, and for the first time in twenty years people felt free to talk in the streets and cafés about the country's social problems and recent exposures of the communist old guard as bureaucratic and corrupt.

Even the deposed Communist Party leader, President Novotny, echoed the new liberal government's view that the last few years had been 'a blot on our postwar existence', referring to the excesses of the security forces.

But the Czech freedoms were not well received across the border in the Soviet Union. Russia today began moving troops and tanks towards the Czech borders with Poland and East Germany. Despite Dubček's assurance of friendship, the Soviets were clearly worried by what was happening in their former puppet state.

Charlie, Reggie and Ronnie Charged With Murder

The three Kray brothers - Charlie, Reggie and Ronnie - were arrested in London today, along with 18 others suspected of conspiracy to murder and fraud, and were officially charged the following day. Two of the brothers, Reggie and Ronnie, were twins, and they in particular had a reputation in London's East End for running a mafia-style operation modelled on Chicago gangsters.

They would be convicted in March 1969, Ronnie being found guilty of two killings and Reggie of one. Sentenced by Mr Justice Melford Stevenson, the twins got life (a minimum of 30 years was recommended) while older brother Charlie was merely convicted of being an accessory. Other gang members also received lighter sentences.

MAY 16

Ronan Point Tower Block Collapses

Modern building techniques were in the spotlight today when a 22-floor block of flats in the east London Borough of Newham was severely damaged by a gas explosion. All 22 apartments on one corner of the so-called 'system-built' Ronan Point tower block (pictured) were demolished and three people were killed.

Some experts believed that the system of building with prefabricated slabs might be to blame and Home Secretary James Callaghan announced that there would be a full inquiry into the incident.

MAY 26

Blues Pioneer Dies Behind Bars

Little Willie John, the American R&B musician and songwriter, died today while serving a sentence for manslaughter in Washington State Penitentiary. Born William Edward John in Camden, Arkansas, in November 1937, Little Willie – he was just five foot four inches tall – had a big talent and an equally noteworthy voice. The Beatles covered his *Leave My Kitten Alone*, Fleetwood Mac would enjoy a hit with *Need Your Love So Bad*, while his 1956 song *Fever* became a much-covered standard. He was survived by his sister, the singer Mabel John, while James Brown - one of many singers influenced by him - would record an album in tribute to his memory.

UK TOP 10 SINGLES

1: What A Wonderful World
- Louis Armstrong

2: Lazy Sunday
- The Small Faces

3: A Man Without Love
- Engelbert Humperdinck

4: Simon Says
- The 1910 Fruitgum Company

5: Young Girl
- Gary Puckett & The Union Gap

6: Can't Take My Eyes Off You
- Andy Williams

7: I Don't Want Our Loving To Die
- The Herd

8: If I Only Had Time
- John Rowles

9: Honey
- Bobby Goldsboro

10: Congratulations
- Cliff Richard

ARRIVALS

Born this month:

9: Neil Ruddock, English football player

28: Kylie Minogue, Australian pop singer, TV and film actress

31: Brian Carey, Republic of Ireland international football player

DEPARTURES

Died this month:

9: 'Judge' George Dewey Hay, compère/host of the Grand Ole Opry country music show 1927-51, aged 73

MAY 22

Parisian Riots Shake Europe And De Gaulle

RIOTING STUDENTS AND STRIKING workers had virtually brought the whole of France to a standstill by the third week of May, in a crisis fit to equal the French Revolution itself. The wave of strikes was prompted by the occupation - by students led by left-wing radical Daniel Cohn-Bendit - of Paris' top place of learning, the Sorbonne University, provoking confrontation with riot police.

By the middle of the month thousands more had joined the protest against the heavy-handedness of the establishment, with the centre of Paris resembling a battlefield. Others marched in support of President Charles de Gaulle, who had been vilified by the left-wingers he believed were trying to grab power.

Hundreds of factories were occupied by workers and the government was forced to raise the minimum wage by 35 per cent. The situation was sufficiently grave for de Gaulle – who dissolved the National Assembly and called a general election to renew his mandate and support his stance – to recall French troops from abroad.

In Britain, students at a number of universities and colleges were sufficiently inspired by events in France to stage sit-ins in protest at what they perceived as academic shortcomings and maladministration of student affairs. In London, action at the London School of Economics was overshadowed by the complete take-over of Hornsey College of Art by students who evicted their principal before barricading themselves inside the building.

Manchester United Win European Cup

Manchester United beat Portugal's Benfica 4-1 in a thrilling Wembley final today to bring soccer's major club prize to Britain for the second year running, Glasgow Celtic having won in Lisbon a year ago. Two goals from Bobby Charlton, and one each from George Best and Brian Kidd, proved more than enough to overwhelm a Benfica team which had forced the game into extra time.

United's appearance in the final was a highly emotional occasion, coming 10 years after the Munich air crash that claimed 23 lives, including eight of the so-called 'Busby Babes', while the team were on European Cup duty.

Manager Matt Busby, who nearly lost his life in Munich, was awarded a knighthood for his services to football. His career crowned, Busby would announce his resignation in January 1969, and eventually die in 1994, still an active member of the United board. It would not be until the appointment as manager of Alex Ferguson, in November 1986, that Busby's record would be even remotely rivalled.

Cannes Film Festival Fracas

French director Jean-Luc Godard effectively closed this year's Cannes Film Festival, barely a week after it had started, when he urged fellow directors to withdraw their films to show solidarity with striking French workers and students. He also suggested that these groups be allowed to see films at no charge. Jury members Roman Polanski, Monica Vitti and Louis Malle resigned in sympathy, and one of the major events of the world movie calendar was left in chaos.

Three Surgery Firsts For UK

Transplant surgery gained three firsts for Britain this month, starting with the first ever liver transplant today, at the Addenbrooke Hospital in Cambridge. The following day, at London's National Heart Hospital, surgeon Donald Ross led the team of 18 doctors and nurses which successfully carried out the UK's first heart transplant, giving a 45 year old man the heart of a 26 year old accident victim.

On May 16, a 15 year old boy, Alex Smith, received a new lung in the first such operation in Britain. Sadly, he was to live only 12 days.

JUNE 6

Bobby Kennedy Killed On Campaign Trail

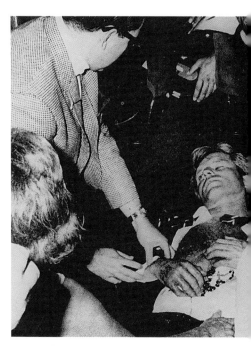

AMERICA WAS IN SHOCK today at the fatal shooting of Senator Robert Kennedy last night in a Los Angeles hotel. Kennedy, younger brother of the assassinated President John F Kennedy, died in the Good Samaritan Hospital after surgeons fought for 20 hours to save his life.

The 43 year old Kennedy had just beaten Senator Eugene McCarthy by taking 50 per cent of the vote in the Democratic Party's California primary election for the presidential nomination, and had just thanked his campaign team at the Ambassador Hotel, when a young Palestinian immigrant, Sirhan Sirhan, fired five shots at point-blank range.

Following the death of Martin Luther King in April, the US had, in the space of a few short weeks, lost two youthful and major influences for liberal reform. And, for the second time in just four and a half years, the Kennedy family prepared to bury one of its sons.

Although conspiracy theorists would devote many years of research into Bobby Kennedy's killing, the fact that the 24 year old assassin shouted 'I did it for my country!' as he was seized by the Senator's aides, suggests that his action was inspired by it being the first anniversary of the Arab-Israeli Six-Day War. Senator Kennedy was a vocal supporter both of Israel and continued US arms supplies to Palestine's sworn enemy.

Robert Fitzgerald Kennedy would be buried at Arlington Cemetery in Washington, alongside the brother he had served as Attorney-General and most trusted confidant. Sirhan Sirhan would be sentenced to a lifetime in prison, as the State of California did not have a death penalty.

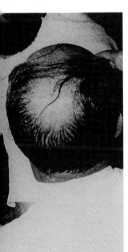

JUNE 1

Helen Keller Dies At 87

The inspirational Helen Keller, whose fortitude in the face of adversity inspired so many, died today at the age of 87. Illness left her both deaf and blind before the age of two, and, while she eventually learned both Braille and sign language, the initial stages of her education were a physical struggle for her teacher Anne Sullivan. This became the subject of a stage play and a hit 1962 film, *The Miracle Worker*, for which Anne Bancroft won a Best Actress Academy Award. Keller graduated with honours from the prestigious Radcliffe College in 1904 and spent her life writing, lecturing and working for the handicapped, her astonishing achievements a constant revelation to those who met her.

JUNE 3

Pop Icon Warhol Attacked

The US Pop Art pioneer Andy Warhol's taste for publicity was indulged to excess today when he was shot and seriously injured by a former colleague, Miss Solanis, who claimed to be the founder of SCUM (the Society for Cutting Up Men). The man who did so much to boost sales for Campbells with his famous painting of a soup can, sustained gunshot injuries to his chest and was rushed to hospital.

Recent years had seen Warhol branching out into unconventional films, and it was in one of these – the, in the circumstances, inappropriately named *I, A Man* – that the disaffected Miss Solanis had appeared.

JUNE 8

Dr King's Assassin Arrested In London

James Earl Ray, the man believed to have murdered the Rev Dr Martin Luther King two months ago, was today arrested at London's Heathrow Airport. The FBI believed that after carrying out the killing in Memphis, Ray travelled to Canada where he obtained a false passport in the name of Ramon George Sneyd, later travelling to London *en route* for Belgium, where he intended to enlist as a mercenary.

Yesterday, Bobby Kennedy's killer Sirhan Sirhan was committed for trial by a Los Angeles jury, as his victim's funeral took place in Washington.

UK TOP 10 SINGLES

1: Young Girl
- Gary Puckett & The Union Gap
2: Honey
- Bobby Goldsboro
3: Jumping Jack Flash
- The Rolling Stones
4: A Man Without Love
- Engelbert Humperdinck
5: This Wheel's On Fire
- Julie Driscoll, Brian Auger & The Trinity
6: Rainbow Valley
- Love Affair
7: Do You Know The Way To San José
- Dionne Warwick
8: Blue Eyes
- Don Partridge
9: Hurdy Gurdy Man
- Donovan
10: I Don't Want Our Loving To Die
- The Herd

ARRIVALS

Born this month:

1: Jason Donovan, Australian TV, film and stage actor, pop singer

8: Neil Mitchell, UK pop musician (Wet Wet Wet)

22: Kingsley Black, Northern Ireland international football player

26: Iwan Roberts, Welsh international football player

28: Adam Woodyatt, UK television actor (*East-Enders*)

DEPARTURES

Died this month:

4: Dorothy Gish (Dorothy de Guiche), US stage and film actress, aged 70

6: Robert Fitzgerald Kennedy, US politician (*see main story*)

7: Dan Duryea, US film actor, aged 61

15: Wes Montgomery, US jazz guitarist, composer, aged 43

17: Frederick West, UK's first heart transplant recipient, aged 45 (*see May news*)

24: Tony Hancock (Anthony John Hancock), UK comedian, actor (*see main story*)

JUNE 5

Mullery's Marching Orders

Alan Mullery, the Tottenham Hotspur midfield player, made history today in the worst possible way when he became the first player ever to be sent off while representing England. Mullery's retaliatory kick at a Yugoslav player who had just brought him down was rewarded both with an over-reaction from his opponent and his marching orders from the referee. Unfortunately, Yugoslavia took advantage of their greater numbers and scored the only goal of the game in the 86th minute through Dzajic.

England thus tumbled out of the European Championships at the semi-final stage, though they beat the Soviet Union three days later to secure third place. Italy in turn beat England's conquerors 2-0 after a replay to secure the Championship on home turf.

JUNE 29

Hyde Park Rocks

The first free rock festival in a series that would extend for several summers, including the famous 1969 Rolling Stones concert to commemorate the death of Brian Jones, was staged today in London's Hyde Park. Pink Floyd were the headliners, and their appearance was eagerly awaited, as they had jettisoned their former lead singer and leading light, Syd Barrett. The move had been anticipated in January, when a second guitarist, David Gilmour, joined to bolster the band's live appearances.

The resulting line-up of Gilmour, Rick Wright (keyboards), Nick Mason (drums) and Roger Waters (bass) topped the bill over Jethro Tull, Tyrannosaurus Rex and Roy Harper, and would endure until Waters quit acrimoniously in 1985. Their output would include landmarks like *Dark Side Of The Moon*, which would sell in excess of 20 million copies.

JUNE 24

Tears For Hancock, Classic Clown

The British comedian Tony Hancock (pictured), whose career had been dogged by setbacks during the past few years, committed suicide today. Trying to stage a comeback on Australian television, he took his own life in a hotel room in Sydney - a sad end for a man who could lay claim to having been one of Britain's most popular and best-loved comedians.

The peak of the 44 year old Hancock's achievement was undoubtedly his 1950s radio programme *Hancock's Half Hour* which was later to cross over to television, where it became one of Britain's most popular series. His character, a lugubrious, snobby and pretentious bungler, made Hancock a true household name and the favourite of millions.

However, subsequent attempts to go it alone - including two poorly-received feature films, *The Rebel* and *The Punch And Judy Man* - flopped badly to begin a downward spiral fuelled by alcoholism, depression and self-doubt. That was sadly misplaced, as continued sales of classic Hancock radio and television episodes to younger generations eloquently prove.

French Voters Give De Gaulle New Mandate

THE PEOPLE OF FRANCE answered President de Gaulle's call for a vote of confidence and a fresh mandate to subdue the turmoil tearing his country apart, today, when his UD-V Party scored a landslide victory in the snap general election and the President found himself with a clear majority over all other political parties combined.

Most satisfying for de Gaulle, whose resignation had been demanded at the height of last month's Paris riots, was the collapse of the Communist Party and the Federation of the Left, whose share of National Assembly seats was cut by more than half.

The election was marred by violence, however. A young Communist supporter was shot dead by men said to be Gaullists, while students erected barricades in the Latin Quarter of Paris and set fire to them as polling-stations opened.

On July 10, Maurice Douve de Murville would be appointed France's new Prime Minister, succeeding Georges Pompidou, a vocal opponent of de Gaulle.

JUNE

POLITICS LOOM AS FOSBURY FLOPS AND BEAMON SOARS IN MEXICO GAMES

It has long been the International Olympic Committee's contention that sport and politics do not mix, but this year's Games - held in Mexico City - marked the first occasion when the Olympic ideal was openly marred by politics. Rioting marked the opening of the so-called 'Friendly Games', while the Games themselves witnessed the expulsion of several black American athletes who used their moments of victory to make political statements.

Forty-nine students were killed by Mexican troops in the riots, while the spirit of protest proclaimed controversially by the 'Black Power' salutes of Tommie Smith and John Carlos, as they stood on the winners' rostrum after being given, respectively, their gold and bronze medals for the 200 metres, was enough to have them put on the next flight home by outraged US team officials.

The rarefied air in Mexico City – which stands at an altitude of 7,000 feet above sea level – produced even more record-breaking times than had been expected or widely predicted. And experts who didn't expect American Bob Beamon's long jump record (almost an

astonishing two feet longer than the previous world best) to be beaten before the end of the twentieth century would only have their predictions disproved in the 1990s, and then by the merest centimetre or two.

But there was no getting away from controversy. If it wasn't politics, it was style. Fortunately, the warnings of US high jumper Dick Fosbury's coach, that there would be dire consequences for anyone trying to emulate the athlete's new and unusual way of clearing the high jump bar, subsequently proved unfounded as a whole generation of jumpers adopted 'The Fosbury Flop' to force the bar higher and higher during the next decades. And it was certainly good news for Fosbury, who won the gold medal with a height of 2.24 metres.

With the Games being beamed back to Europe via satellite for the first time, news or coverage of two British victories reached home faster than ever before. The only gold medals to head back to Heathrow Airport would be carried by middleweight boxer Chris Finnegan and 400m hurdler David Hemery, although there would be silver medals in the baggage of 400m runner Lilian Board (just

Dick Fosbury

beaten by France's Colette Besson) and long jumper Sheila Sherwood.

Just as victory in the light heavyweight final of the 1960 Rome Olympics had acted as a superb springboard for the young American boxer called Cassius Clay, and Tokyo had done likewise for Joe Frazier in 1964, so Mexico would give another big US fighter and future professional world champion his calling card when he decided to go knocking on potential managers' doors.

The heavyweight silver medal went to the Soviet Union's Iomas Chepulis, but the gold to a 20 year old from Marshall, Texas. His name? George Foreman.

JULY 2

David Owen Joins UK Government

There was a fresh new face in the British Government today when 30 year old Dr David Owen, a trained physician, became the youngest member of the Labour Party cabinet. Just over two years after taking his seat in the Commons as the new MP for Plymouth, the young politician with the dashing good looks was given the job of Under-Secretary for the Navy.

Eight years later Owen would become the youngest Foreign Secretary the country had seen for 40 years. He would, however, leave the Labour Party in the 1980s to form the Social Democrats, and their subsequent absorption into the Liberal Democrats saw his power fade. In the 1990s, as Lord Owen, he would be appointed the UN's principal envoy and negotiator charged with trying to settle the war in former Yugoslavia.

Lone Yachtsman Alec Rose Returns Home

JUST THIRTEEN MONTHS after Sir Francis Chichester made landfall at Plymouth to complete the first ever solo circumnavigation of the world, 59 year old Alec Rose (pictured) returned to his home city of Portsmouth having also accomplished the 28,500-mile voyage single-handed.

But while Sir Francis had taken just 226 days to make the voyage, Rose – sailing in a ketch named *Lively Lady* – took 354 days. The amateur sailor - he was actually a greengrocer - admitted that his attempt had almost failed on the New Zealand-Cape Horn leg of the trip when he hit mountainous seas and hurricane-force winds.

Safely home despite his ordeal, Rose was greeted by a crowd of 250,000 as he set foot on English soil once more, his achievement rewarded by his being made a Freeman of the City of Portsmouth.

'Humanae Vitae' Says 'No' To Birth Control

Pope Paul made a firm stand against the social climate of the times today when the leader of the world's 530 million Catholics announced that there would be no relaxation in the Vatican's position on artificial contraception.

The latest Papal encyclical which has been named *Humanae Vitae (Of Human Life)* would not find complete favour with many liberal Catholics who'd hoped for a relaxation of previous hard-line pronouncements which opened the way for transgressors to be excommunicated.

It certainly had profound implications for the millions of Catholics living in poor countries who could ill afford the problems caused by the ban on birth control.

UK TOP 10 SINGLES

1: Baby Come Back
- The Equals
2: I Pretend
- Des O'Connor
3: Son Of Hickory Hollers Tramp
- OC Smith
4: Yesterday Has Gone
- Cupid's Inspiration
5: Yummy Yummy Yummy
- Ohio Express
6: Mony Mony
- Tommy James & The Shondells
7: Jumping Jack Flash
- The Rolling Stones
8: My Name Is Jack
- Manfred Mann
9: MacArthur Park
- Richard Harris
10: Blue Eyes
- Don Partridge

Leading Rock Groups Go Pop

Legendary British blues group The Yardbirds split up today, leaving guitarist Jimmy Page with obligations to fulfil in the shape of Scandinavian dates. He would rename his New Yardbirds, Led Zeppelin, after Who drummer Keith Moon's dismissive description of their crowd-pleasing potential.

Three days later, former Yardbirds guitarist Eric Clapton (who, with Jeff Beck, had found early fame in their ranks) announced that his current band, Cream, were to break up due to a 'loss of direction'. Manager Robert Stigwood confirmed the decision three days later, stating that there would be a farewell tour later in the year.

DEPARTURES
Died this month:
21: Ruth St Denis, American dancer, choreographer, aged 90
28: Otto Hahn, German nuclear physicist, aged 88 (*see main story*)

TV Hit Goes Back To The War

THE CREDITS ROLLED for the first time tonight on *Dad's Army*, a television show totally out of step with the Swinging Sixties, but one which was to become a British institution over the next nine years. The fictional but believable exploits of a motley crew of reservists in World War II commanded by a bumbling bank manager Captain and a vague, upper-class Sergeant, captured the imagination not only of those who could remember the war but a younger generation for whom the stereotypes with a twist struck a chord.

The show's principal actors - Arthur Lowe, John Le Mesurier, Clive Dunn, Ian Lavender and Arnold Ridley - lent warmth and credibility to their often-inept characters, while catch-phrases such as 'Permission to speak, sir', 'Stupid boy' and 'We're doomed' rapidly became familiar nationwide.

Writers Jimmy Perry and David Croft would go on to create other hit comedies, most notably *It Ain't Half Hot Mum* (another WWII series, this time set in India) and the holiday camp-set *Hi De Hi*, but neither would prove as enduring or as endearing as their tales of the mismatched heroes of the Walminton-on-Sea Home Guard.

Nuclear Pioneer Dies

Otto Hahn, the man responsible for one of the most important scientific discoveries of the twentieth century - a way of achieving nuclear fission - died today at the age of 88. After studying in England and Canada, Hahn returned to his native Germany in the first decade of the century, where he continued research work into radioactivity.

His most valuable work was accomplished in the pre-World War II years when, in collaboration with Lise Meitner and Fritz Strassmann, he proved the feasibility of nuclear fission. Thankfully, the weapon applications of the new discovery were not appreciated by the Nazi Party and Hahn spent the war years working on nuclear-powered energy programmes.

Flag-Burning Not So Nice

Classical-rock fusion outfit The Nice were tonight banned from appearing ever again at London's Royal Albert Hall where, with a dramatic display of anti-Vietnam War sentiment, they burned and stamped on the Stars and Stripes.

The action accompanied keyboard player Keith Emerson's adaptation of Leonard Bernstein's *America* (from the musical *West Side Story*). Emerson would later expand on these theatrics - which included stabbing his Hammond organ with knives - as a member of the internationally successful Emerson Lake and Palmer in the 1970s.

JULY 6

Laver And King Triumph At First Open Wimbledon

The decision to end the distinction between amateur and professional players at the Wimbledon Tennis Championships was a winner as far as Rod Laver (pictured) and Billie-Jean King were concerned, as both emerged as champions in contests which really did feature the world's best players.

After being forced to stay away for the six years since he went professional, the flame-haired Australian made a convincing reappearance when he beat fellow-Australian Tony Roche in the final in straight sets, 6-3, 6-4, 6-2. Californian women's ace Billie-Jean King notched up another Women's Singles win - her third - when she stopped the tall Judy Tegart from making it an Australian double in two sets. She was the first woman since Maureen 'Little Mo' Connolly to win the title three times in succession.

Russian Tanks Smash Prague Spring

THE SOVIET UNION today moved to crush the fragile flower of freedom in Czechoslovakia, closing down television and radio stations, occupying the country's National Assembly in Prague and taking its leader, Alexander Dubček, prisoner. But with only a brief taste of freedom after years of oppression the Czech people were not taking the Russian invasion lying down.

Huge crowds tried to reason with Soviet tank crews – and when that failed they took to the streets with guns and sticks. But with troops supported by superior Soviet air power, the result was a foregone conclusion. Thirty Czechs were reported to have been killed in the first few hours of the invasion, and many more wounded.

The Soviet action - a tragic echo of the Red Army's demolition of Hungary's bid for reform in 1956 - took Dubček and his principal supporters by surprise. So confident was he that the Moscow regime was prepared to reach some sort of compromise, he had been involved in high-level talks only hours before the tanks rolled in.

When news of the invasion was broken to him in a telephone call, Dubček was reportedly stunned, crying out, 'Why have they done this to me? My entire life has been devoted to co-operation with the Soviet Union!'

The Prague Spring was over, and the recriminations - and punishments - could begin to drag Czechoslovakia back to its previous, Soviet-dominated state.

Thousands Starve In Biafra War

The Nigerian blockade of rebellious Biafra reached serious proportions with thousands going short of food in the region torn apart by civil war. Peace negotiations being held today in the Ethiopian capital of Addis Ababa made little progress, with Biafra fearing that a return to Nigerian rule would mean a resumption of the massacres which prompted Biafra's declaration of independence last year. The Red Cross was drawing up plans for an air-lift of food supplies to save the population from starvation.

Goons Go On And On

On the 21st anniversary of their formation in the Grafton Arms public house in Victoria, London, British comedy team The Goons reunited tonight for a one-off TV special entitled *A Tale of Men's Shirts*.
Original Goons Peter Sellers, Spike Milligan and Harry Secombe were joined by John Cleese, taking the place of founder-member Michael Bentine, who left the team in 1954. Tonight's show pulled in 5.5 million viewers – more than respectable for a cult show whose medium had always been radio. Prince Charles, a long-time Goons fan who once bought some of the show's original scripts, was doubtless among them.

Nixon Gains Republican Nomination

Richard Nixon, the man who only narrowly failed to beat John F Kennedy in the 1960 US Presidential election, was adopted as the Republican Party's candidate once more today, at the party's Miami convention. Nixon, who served as President Dwight D Eisenhower's Vice-President from 1952 to 1960, in turn chose the right-wing Governor of Maryland, Spiro T Agnew, as his Vice-Presidential running mate - a move which surprised moderates within the Party.

Agnew had strong views on law and order – sure to be a big election issue in the current domestic situation – and had no time for anti-war demonstrators whom he branded an 'effete corps of impudent snobs'.

UK TOP 10 SINGLES

1: Mony Mony
- Tommy James & The Shondells
2: Fire
- The Crazy World Of Arthur Brown
3: This Guy's In Love With You
- Herb Alpert
4: I Pretend
- Des O'Connor
5: I Close My Eyes And Count To Ten
- Dusty Springfield
6: Help Yourself
- Tom Jones
7: Mrs Robinson
- Simon & Garfunkel
8: Sunshine Girl
- Herman's Hermits
9: Dance To The Music
- Sly & The Family Stone
10: Do It Again
- The Beach Boys

ARRIVALS

Born this month:
11: Alan Kelly, Republic of Ireland international football player
16: Dmitri Kharine, CIS international football player
31: Derek Whyte, Scotland international football player

DEPARTURES

Died this month:
22: Kay Francis (Katherine Gibbs), US film actress (*Street Of Chance, The White Angel*), aged 69

AUGUST 29

Violence Erupts At Democratic Convention

ONLY A WEEK AFTER television viewers in the US had watched the Soviet invasion of Czechoslovakia and consoled themselves with the assumption that nothing similar could happen in their country, they witnessed the sight of hundreds of Chicago riot police on the rampage outside the Democratic Party's convention.

Their intended targets were anti-war protesters whom Chicago's Mayor Richard Daley had ordered to be cleared away from the city centre. But it was all too clear, as the major news organizations broadcast live coverage of the carnage, that many innocent young children and old people were among those who were mercilessly whipped, beaten or attacked with Mace gas.

The police riot, which one Democrat delegate angrily described as 'Gestapo tactics', even reached the convention floor when two other delegates were dragged, screaming and shouting, out of the hall by helmeted officers. The majority of those injured were peace marchers heading towards the convention from a camp they'd established in the city's Grant Park.

The atmosphere within the convention hall darkened to deeper despair for many when, with the assassinated Bobby Kennedy out of the running, the right-wing Senator Hubert Humphrey won the Party's nomination for the Presidency, beating the only surviving liberal, George McGovern. The more radical elements within the Party believed that Humphrey's position on Vietnam was indistinguishable from that of the Republican Party.

AUGUST 22

Beatle Wife Bows Out

Cynthia Lennon, wife of John, the first member of The Beatles to marry, today sued her husband for divorce. He had been living for some while with the Japanese singer-artist Yoko Ono, whom he had met in November 1966 and who would become his second wife.

The Lennon's six-year marriage would finally end in November, the same month that Yoko would miscarry John's baby.

Julian Lennon, born to John and Cynthia in 1963, would later become a singing star in his own right, while Cynthia would write a best-selling autobiography, *A Twist Of Lennon,* the title neatly combining her two married surnames.

Mariner 6 Reaches Mars

The US space probe, *Mariner 6*, which had been launched by NASA on February 24, today became the latest in the Mariner programme - which was designed to explore all the planets of the solar system - to send back data.

Previous Mariner probes had explored the planet Venus, but *Mariner 6* was sending back photographs and data on Mars following experiments to analyze the planet's atmosphere, size and surface.

Mariner 4, which had passed by the planet in July 1965, had given scientists their first ever close-up of the Red Planet, but the information from *Mariner 6* would prove much more detailed and instructive.

El Al Hijack Is Over

The hijack drama of the Israeli El Al jet which began on July 23 ended peacefully today when the last 12 Jewish hostages were released by the Palestinian terrorists who'd been demanding the release of prisoners taken by Israel in last year's Arab-Israeli Six-Day War.

The hostages' 40-day ordeal had begun when the terrorists seized the jet, which was on its way from Rome to Tel Aviv, and ordered the pilot to fly to Algiers. All non-Israeli passengers were then released by the men, who claimed to be members of the Popular Front for the Liberation of Palestine. An end to the siege was negotiated by the Red Cross.

King Elvis Returns With Back-To-Roots TV Smash

The announcement, in January this year, that the Singer Sewing Machine Company was to sponsor the first-ever Elvis Presley TV special for NBC-TV, may have thrilled the former King of Rock 'n' Roll's still-loyal fans to bits, but didn't exactly set the rest of us dancing with unbridled joy.

Since returning to civilian life in 1960, the man who'd personified the dangerous edge of early rock 'n' roll had submerged himself in an unending string of movies noted mostly for their unrelenting mediocrity, and a recording career which only rarely produced anything special.

As it happened, the simply-titled *Elvis* would, when it finally reached US TV screens in December, prove an undiluted thrill and a revelation as Presley devoted most of the proceedings to excerpts from informal and astonishingly good jam sessions producer Steve Binder had filmed in front of invited audiences in June.

With a semi-acoustic band consisting of long-time musical buddies Scotty Moore (on guitar), Charlie Hodge (on bass) and drummer DJ Fontana, Presley returned to his rock 'n' roll, country, blues and gospel roots. No hip-shaking, no big-star showing off, just four friends recapturing lost glories and good times as they sat around on stools.

Even the big production numbers, when Presley left that intimate gathering to strut his stuff with dancers and gaudy sets, were treated with a wry good humour which suggested that Elvis thought they were pretty dumb too. But the one-hour show's finale, the dramatic *If I Can Dream*, would give him his biggest US chart hit for years when it was released as a single in January next year.

Unfortunately, The King had not returned to claim his crown. He soon drifted back to making more of those terrible movies and a Las Vegas persona which deteriorated into rhinestone kitsch.

FAME COMES TOO LATE FOR TRAGIC OTIS

One of the sensations of the 1967 Monterey Pop Festival when he, Jimi Hendrix and Janis Joplin poleaxed a vast crowd of rock fans with their music and energy, it is tragically ironic that the international success achieved by Otis Redding's single *(Sittin' On) The Dock Of The Bay* came too late for the gifted young soul star. He and members of his touring band, The Bar Kays, had been killed on December 10 last year when their aircraft crashed.

US rock fans' 'discovery' of the 27 year old, Georgia-born Redding should have enabled him to repeat the huge popularity he had, in fact, enjoyed for the past two years in Britain and Europe, where he and various other artists who recorded for the small but influential Stax Records label in Memphis, were subjects of the kind of idol worship usually reserved for white rock stars.

Signed to Stax in late 1962, Redding's way with a song - whether it was a tortured ballad or a tight, funky up-tempo number - was soon giving him US R&B chart hits and the start of that European legend. *These Arms Of Mine, Pain In My Heart, Mr Pitiful, I've Been Loving You Too Long (To Stop Now)* and *Respect* all contributed to that reputation. When he and a revue of Stax artists toured Britain and Europe in 1966, Redding had the rare distinction of having an entire edition of the influential British TV show *Ready, Steady, Go!* given over to him and his music.

The R&B chart hits continued (as did UK and European success) with *My Girl, Satisfaction, My Lover's Prayer, Fa-Fa-Fa-Fa-Fa (Sad Song)* and *Try A Little Tenderness*, so when he was invited to replace The Beach Boys on the Monterey Pop bill in June last year, he had a formidable back catalogue to draw on for his first major rock gig in the US.

Recorded only days before his death, *(Sittin' On) The Dock Of The Bay* would race to the top of the US pop charts in January this year and stay there for four weeks, selling well over a million copies in the process. An eventual No 3 UK hit and a Top 10 single in many other countries, it would trigger the re-release of all his albums and the compilation of innumerable 'Best Of' collections, sales of which proved how universal his appeal was, and reinforcing the tragedy that he had not survived to build on that appeal.

DIANA STEPS FORWARD TO REIGN SUPREME

The change of billing - from 'The Supremes' to 'Diana Ross and The Supremes' - had first appeared on the Motown trio's *Reflections* single in August 1967, but it was during this year that it became clear that the Detroit-based label had decided to push the delectable Miss Ross towards an eventual solo career.

As they progressed through 1968 - a relatively quiet year in terms of releases and hits, with *Love Child* and *I'm Gonna Make You Love Me* their only US Top 20 entries - the group concentrated on an extensive concert schedule which included a short season at London's Talk of the Town, where Paul McCartney, Michael Caine and Cliff Richard were spotted in the audience and were undoubtedly featured on the applause tracks of their best-selling UK album *Live At London's Talk of the Town*.

In November Ross, Mary Wilson and newcomer Cindy Birdsong appeared before the Queen at the annual Royal

Otis Redding

Variety Show, with Diana's between-songs plea for racial tolerance winning huge applause.

The year ended on a high when the *Diana Ross and The Supremes Meet The Temptations* album shot to No 2 in the US LP charts, and although 1969 would deliver more hits for the group, no-one was in any doubt that she and her colleagues had reached the parting of the ways which would actually come about in 1970.

SEPT

Outrage As South Africa Bans MCC Player

THE APARTHEID REGIME in South Africa reacted swiftly today following the announcement that the South African-born all-rounder Basil d'Oliveira (pictured) was included in the MCC side for a prospective cricket tour of their country. The tour was cancelled, creating outrage throughout the sporting world and setting South Africa on a collision course with the international community.

Prime Minister John Vorster made the startling claim that the MCC was 'no longer a cricket team, but a team of troublemakers', so establishing the tone of increasingly hostile dealings as fruitless attempts were made to reconcile differences.

Ironically, d'Oliveira - who originally left South Africa because of racist laws which classified him, a mixed-race man, as a so-called Cape Coloured with no civil rights and unable to play alongside lesser white players - had not been included in the touring party at first, a decision which had caused controversy in Britain where it was viewed as a back-down. But when bowler Tom Cartwright was found to be unfit, d'Oliveira was back in, and the tour was off.

The MCC establishment had managed, in a few short weeks, to outrage the anti-apartheid lobby by not including d'Oliveira, and the South African apartheid regime when they decided to add him to their touring party!

UK TOP 10 SINGLES

1: I've Gotta Get A Message To You
- The Bee Gees
2: Do It Again
- The Beach Boys
3: I Say A Little Prayer
- Aretha Franklin
4: Hold Me Tight
- Johnny Nash
5: Hey Jude
- The Beatles
6: Those Were The Days
- Mary Hopkin
7: This Guy's In Love With You
- Herb Alpert
8: High In The Sky
- Amen Corner
9: Help Yourself
- Tom Jones
10: Jesamine
- The Casuals

SEPTEMBER 11

New Technique Revolutionizes Childbirth

The ideal of painfree childbirth came a step closer today when a new form of anaesthesia was announced in London. Called the 'epidural technique', it consisted of an injection of anaesthetic into the membrane around the spine during labour, causing a loss of sensation from the waist down.

Because the needle could be kept in place during the birth, the pain relief could be topped up when required.

First indications were that mothers-to-be welcomed the discovery, which would go on to be recognized as the most effective pain relief method – though natural childbirth enthusiasts were against it.

SEPTEMBER 14

Hey, Jude Is Apple To The Core

The Beatles' latest single *Hey Jude* hit the No 1 spot in Britain's charts today. But their 15th chart-topper was different to its predecessors, appearing not on the Parlophone imprint of EMI Records, but the group's own Apple label. At seven minutes and 11 seconds long, it also set a record as the longest single to ever reach No 1, while its entry into the US *Billboard* listings on this very day was at No 10, the highest first chart position any single had registered to this date.

Writer Paul McCartney claimed the song was inspired by John Lennon's son Julian, changing 'Jules' to 'Jude'. The four-minute fade-out, with its 'na na-na' chorus, was immediately distinctive. US soul star Wilson Pickett would also chart, albeit less spectacularly, with his own version of the song later in the year.

SEPTEMBER 27

Britain Drops Stage Censorship, 'Hair' Cast Drop Clothes!

ON THE FIRST DAY of the Britain's new liberalized stage censorship laws, the 13-member cast of the musical *Hair* (pictured) shed their clothes in front of the capacity audience attending the London première of the US stage musical about to move to Broadway.

The show's title song was a eulogy to the symbolic freedom of long, unfettered hair as sported by every self-respecting hippie, while the show itself featured trendy psychedelic lighting, loud music and swearing, rounded off with the final let-it-all-hang-out nude scene.

Until today, when the task of censoring all play scripts (with the power to demand cuts, or inflict an all-out ban) was taken from the Lord Chamberlain's office, leaving possible litigation to more sensitive members of theatre audiences, the *Hair* cast could not have acted the way they did.

SEPTEMBER 28

Domingo Makes New York Début

Spanish-born opera singer Placido Domingo made his first appearance on the stage of the New York Metropolitan Opera tonight - four days earlier than expected, when he was called on to replace Franco Corelli at short notice.

Although Domingo started his singing career as a baritone in his parents' company, he had gained the reputation of being one of the world's premier lyric tenors in the past few years.

Domingo's New York Met début was to mark the beginning of a long association with the company, during which time he would sing more than 30 different roles.

SEPTEMBER 8

Virginia Wade Wins US Open

Britain's leading lady tennis player, 23 year old Virginia Wade, beat hot favourite Billie-Jean King to become the first winner of the new US Open Tennis Championship today. America's Arthur Ashe took the honours in the men's tournament.

Wade, the daughter of a clergyman, was born in Bournemouth, England, but had lived as a child in South Africa. She would gain further fame in 1977 when she won the Wimbledon title, a popular choice as a home-grown champion in the Queen's Jubilee Year. She would go on to become a media commentator after her retirement.

SEPTEMBER 19

Birth Of Heavy Metal

The US rock group Steppenwolf, fronted by East German émigré John Kay, struck gold today when their single *Born To Be Wild* was certified a million-seller. The track was included on their eponymous début album, which followed its example and turned gold in November. The high-octane track, which would gain a new lease of life when included on the soundtrack of the cult movie *Easy Rider* in 1969, was also credited with popularizing the term 'heavy metal' which appeared in its lyric, though it had also appeared in the William Burroughs novel *Naked Lunch*.

SEPTEMBER 8

Xerox Inventor Fades Out

American inventor Chester Floyd Carlson, died today at the age of 62. His most famous invention was eventually to affect every corner of the world, revolutionizing working practices as the photocopying machine became a fixture in every office.

So effective was the marketing of Carlson's new machine that 'xeroxing' became a generic name for the photocopying process, just as 'hoovering' did for everyone cleaning their carpets, whether or not they used a vacuum cleaner made by the Hoover company.

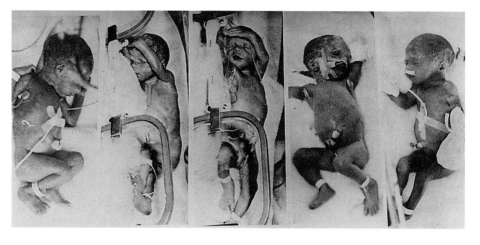

OCTOBER 26

Sextuplets Born To British 'Fertility Drug' Mother

THE HAZARDS OF NEW so-called 'fertility drugs' being prescribed to women who'd experienced problems in becoming pregnant were made manifestly clear in Birmingham's Maternity Hospital today when Sheila Ann Thorns - a local patient who'd received the aids to conception - gave birth to Britain's first sextuplets.

One of the babies, a girl, died soon after birth, leaving Mrs Thorns with two sons and three daughters (pictured), all of them born two months prematurely by Caesarean section.

The babies' arrival was a complete surprise to their grandmother - Mrs Thorns and her husband had kept her pregnancy secret even from their families. Asked about the obvious problem of multiple births when fertility drugs were involved, a specialist said that the clinic team would be 'guarding against any similar occurrence in the future'.

Mao - China Well And Truly Purged

In a recent rare admission of error which finally reached Western media today, Chinese leader Mao Tse-tung made clear his disappointment at the actions of Red Guard leaders throughout the Cultural Revolution. 'You have let me down, and you have disappointed the workers, peasants and soldiers of China', the Communist Party Chairman was reported as saying, referring to the widespread violence and chaos caused by the over-zealous activities of the Guard throughout the last two and a half years.

Although the Cultural Revolution - which Mao had started to instil a fresh vigour in China - had resulted in factions of the Red Guard fighting each other over ideological differences, Mao was still claiming it had been a success. However, it was clear that the army still remained Chairman Mao's only hope of restoring order to his shell-shocked and financially ruined country.

Beatle Bust Hits Headlines

John Lennon and his partner Yoko Ono were today arrested for possessing cannabis, the police raid on Beatle drummer Ringo Starr's London flat - where the couple were staying - embarrassingly coinciding with the world première of Lennon's film début, *How I Won The War*.

On November 28, Lennon would become the first Beatle to be arraigned on drugs charges, when he was fined £150 for possession. The court accepted his explanation that he no longer smoked the substance and that the quantity found was an old, long-forgotten stash.

Although Yoko Ono was cleared and the fine was nominal, the after-effects of the conviction would explode in the mid-1970s when Lennon was refused US residency on the grounds of having a drug record and was forced to mount an eventually-successful campaign to remain in New York.

Sad Dubček Admits Defeat

The Soviet clampdown on Czechoslovakia's recently-found freedoms continued this month, following the re-imposition of press censorship last month, the prohibition of meetings likely to 'endanger socialism', and the resignation of Foreign Minister Jiri Halek.

The announcement that Warsaw Pact troops would be staying in Czechoslovakia was greeted with dismay by the Czechs, tens of thousands of whom would march through the capital, Prague, on October 28 to protest against the continued occupation.

Alexander Dubček remained First Secretary of the Czech Communist Party, but when he arrived back in Czechoslovakia from Moscow today he had been forced to concede to Soviet demands to abandon his political reforms in favour of a resumption of the old ways.

UK TOP 10 SINGLES

1: Those Were The Days
- Mary Hopkin

2: Hey Jude
- The Beatles

3: Jesamine
- The Casuals

4: Little Arrows
- Leapy Lee

5: Lady Willpower
- Gary Puckett & The Union Gap

6: My Little Lady
- The Tremeloes

7: Red Balloon
- The Dave Clark Five

8: A Day Without Love
- Love Affair

9: Hold Me Tight
- Johnny Nash

10: Les Bicyclettes De Belsize
- Engelbert Humperdinck

Born this month:
2: Philip Gray, Northern Ireland international football player
14: Matthew Le Tissier, England international football player
17: Graeme Le Saux, England international football player;
Ziggy Marley, Jamaican singer-songwriter, musician
31: Alistair McErlaine, UK pop musician (Texas)

DEPARTURES

Died this month:
1: Marcel Duchamp, French artist, aged 81
11: George White, US stage producer, aged 78
13: Sir Stanley Unwin, UK book publisher, aged 83
18: Lee Tracy, US film actor (*Doctor X, Dinner At Eight*, etc), aged 70
20: Bud Flanagan (Chaim Reeven Weintrop), UK comedian, singer (*Underneath The Arches*, etc), member of The Crazy Gang, aged 72

OCTOBER 6

Troops Break Up Catholic Demo In Londonderry

An estimated 100 Roman Catholic demonstrators were reported injured in Londonderry tonight as riot police moved in to break up two days and nights of bloody street battles and a march in defiance of a ban imposed by Ulster's Home Affairs Minister, William Craig.

The demonstrations, against sectarian discrimination in employment and housing, involved local Catholic church leaders, students and trade unionists, and were ended when armoured cars, baton charges and high-pressure water hoses were used by British troops.

OCTOBER 18

UK Supergroups Hit The Stage

This month saw the birth of not one, but two future British rock institutions, as Led Zeppelin - the group formed by ex-Yardbirds guitarist Jimmy Page - played their first low-key UK date at London's Marquee Club tonight. While Zeppelin's multi-platinum career would end with the death of drummer John Bonham in 1980, the main protagonists, Page and vocalist Robert Plant, would reconvene as a duo in 1994 to continue the story.

The day after Zep took their bow, the seeds of Humble Pie were sown when top pop group The Herd's guitarist and singer Pete Frampton jammed with The Small Faces' guitarist/singer Steve Marriott. The duo would unite to form Humble Pie, leaving the remaining Small Faces to recruit guitarist Ron Wood and singer Rod Stewart as Marriott's replacement, dropping the 'Small' in the process.

OCTOBER 20

Jackie K Marries Aristotle O

DESPITE THE FACT that it was now five years since the brutal assassination of her first husband, President John F Kennedy, in Dallas, Jacqueline Kennedy's marriage to Greek shipping magnate Aristotle Onassis (pictured with Jackie's daughter Caroline Kennedy) surprised many of her loyal devotees and stunned the world.

'Jackie K' was the darling of the American public in the early years of the decade, displaying, as she did, impeccable taste in dress and manners and bravely enduring the tragic deaths of her baby and her husband.

Her remarriage to the much older and ostentatiously-wealthy Onassis, who'd made his fortune capitalizing on the Allies need for cargo ships during World War II, sparked off worldwide media interest.

According to Jackie, the big day was just 'the happiest day of my life' - a remark calculated to alienate her from a US public which still held the memory of their dead President in something akin to unquestioning awe.

Booker Competition Launched

A new prize for fiction writing in Britain was announced jointly today by the multi-national conglomerate Booker McConnell and the Publishers' Association. The first award of the Booker Prize, as it came to be known, which carried a £5,000 prize, would be awarded for the best full-length British novel published in 1968.

The sponsors were aiming to give British writers an equal incentive to that offered by the French Prix Goncourt, which stimulated a considerable amount of public interest. Like the Goncourt, the Booker would also provide Britain's chattering classes with more than their fair share of controversy in coming years as hotly tipped books failed to win, and unfancied outsiders romped home.

OCT

KYLIE MINOGUE - FROM CHILD STAR TO POP DIVA

There was nothing in her family background to suggest that Kylie Minogue's life would take the course it did. Born today in Melbourne, Australia, her father was an accountant while her Welsh-extraction mother was apparently content to fill her time as a house-maker for him, Kylie (the name is Aboriginal and is what native Australians call the boomerang) and her sister Dannii.

However, by the age of 11 Kylie had successfully auditioned for a part in the top Australian soap drama *The Sullivans* (she played a Dutch girl), and followed that, later in 1979, by winning a longer-running role in another series, *Skyways* - which also featured a young actor called Jason Donovan.

Completing her high school education, Kylie pitched herself full-time into an acting career with parts in three more soaps, *The Hendersons*, *Fame And Misfortune* and *The Zoo Family*, before accepting the role which would change her life - that of Charlene in the recently-launched daily show *Neighbours* - in 1986. One of the other youngsters who enlivened proceedings in the fictional Melbourne suburban Ramsey Street was her chum Jason, with whom she was destined to have an on-screen romance and eventual marriage which would take them away from the series.

That was all in the future, however, as Kylie became one of the most popular characters in what had quickly become Australia's most popular series, her performance winning her the prestigious Logie Award in 1987. That was the year when, while a guest of honour at an Australian Rules Football game in Sydney, Kylie was

persuaded to sing for the crowd. Vamping a version of the Little Eva oldie *The Locomotion* to wild applause, she was offered a recording contract, recorded the song for real and watched as it hit No 1 in the Australian charts and stayed there for seven weeks!

With *The Locomotion* a hit in New Zealand and many Far East countries and *Neighbours* now running in Britain on BBC Television (and attracting 14 million viewers every day), Kylie - in London for a promotional visit - was approached by pop producer Pete Waterman who easily persuaded her to let him work with her. The first result of their collaboration was *I Should Be So Lucky* which, when it was released in January 1988, really did change Kylie's life.

By February it was Britain's No 1 single, had also hit the top in Australia (where Kylie was being given four further Logie Awards), and would go on to head the charts in 12 other countries. In May, the follow-up *Got To Be Certain* reached the No 2 spot in Britain, while the July release of her début album *Kylie* saw it enter the UK charts at No 1 and qualify for a platinum disc with more than a million sales.

Meanwhile, a re-mixed *The Locomotion* entered the British charts at No 2, confirming Kylie as the most successful female débutane in history - especially when the single hit No 3 in the US in November and it was confirmed that only Barbra Streisand and Madonna had managed to precede her in making albums which were the best-selling in their respective years.

Having, with Jason Donovan, made her farewells to *Neighbours*, Kylie and he teamed up to record the UK January 1989 No 1 hit duet *Especially For You* while Kylie's solo single *It's No Secret* peaked at No 37 in the US. May saw her back at the top of the UK charts with *Hand On Your Heart*, while the August UK No 2 she had with *Wouldn't Change A Thing* made it seven-in-a-row singles which had hit either No 1 or No 2 in Britain.

A second Waterman-produced album repeated the feat of the first in every detail, and Kylie managed to juggle her increasingly tight schedule, which was now including world concert tours, to return to acting and an appearance in the Australian-produced film *The Delinquents*.

In 1990, having scored more huge international hits with *Tears On My Pillow*, *Better The Devil You Know* and *Step Back In Time*, Kylie decided to make a break with Pete Waterman and tread her own musical path. Her decision was undoubtedly influenced by a relationship she had with Michael Hutchence, lead singer with Australian rock band INXS, but has led to her emerging as a sophisticated, witty and adventurous performer, still capable of scoring major hits, but now very much her own woman.

JASON DONOVAN - ANY DREAM WILL DO

Unlike his *Neighbours* co-star and fictional love interest, Kylie Minogue, Jason Donovan - who was born today in the Melbourne suburb of Malvern - had every reason to consider an acting career as 'normal'. His father is Terence Donovan, one of Australia's best-known TV and film actors, while his mother, Sue McIntosh, is an equally well-known TV presenter.

In 1988, as Kylie's pop career went into overdrive, Jason travelled to London to record two songs with the production team headed by Kylie's producer, Pete Waterman. That September, his first single, *Nothing Can Divide Us*, was released and became the country's No 5 hit. Now a genuine teen idol in Britain, Jason's next solo single, *Too Many Broken Hearts* became the UK's No 1 single, and his decision to switch his career to the UK and music was justified in May when his first album *Ten Good Reasons* topped the British charts and sold more than a million copies. During that year Jason would score further UK Top 10 hits, while 1990 would see him chart with *Hang On To Your Love*, *Another Night*, *Rhythm Of The Rain*, *I'm Doing Fine* and *RSVP* as his second album, *Between The Lines*, entered the UK charts at No 2.

Aware that the teen idol phase was likely to end before long, Jason made a brave decision agreeing to star in a major London revival of the Tim Rice-Andrew Lloyd Webber musical *Joseph And His Amazing Technicolor Dreamcoat*.

It was a smash, and Jason found himself back at No 1 in the UK singles charts when *Any Dream Will Do*, a song from the show, was released. Proving himself a shrewd strategic planner, Jason would not over stay his welcome in the show and left it after a heady six months, returning - in the main - to his acting career, which he continues with some distinction in a commendably wide variety of roles.

NOVEMBER 1

LBJ Orders End To Vietnam Bombing

IN WHAT WOULD PROVE to be one of the last decisions of his Presidency, Lyndon Johnson today announced that he had ordered the cessation of all bombing by US forces on targets in North Vietnam. He made it clear in his televised speech that he hoped this move would facilitate progress in the Paris peace talks.

There was an early indication that the North Vietnamese regime in Hanoi saw Johnson's gesture in that same spirit as it finally agreed to allow the South Vietnamese Government to participate in the talks.

Back in the US, however, many cynics believed the announcement was made to boost Vice-President Hubert Humphrey's position in the final run-up to the presidential elections. While pollsters reported a late surge in Humphrey's fortunes, Johnson's move - if it was a calculated election ploy - would prove too little, too late.

NOVEMBER 14

Maggie And Shirley Strike Blows For Women

Two women - very different in background and future careers - struck heavy and telling blows for women's roles in politics this month.

On November 5, Shirley Chisholm became the first black woman to win election to the US House of Representatives.

In future global terms, the more telling blow was made today by Margaret Thatcher, destined to be the future first woman Prime Minister of Britain. She put her first foot on the ladder to political fame and fortune when she was appointed Shadow Transport Minister by Conservative Party leader Edward Heath, the man she would eventually oust to begin her last push to the very top of international status.

Forsyte Back For Second Bite

One of 1968's biggest British television hits was a repeat. Nothing strange in that, but *The Forsyte Saga* had only been broadcast for the first time a year earlier!

The drama series - based on the Victorian novels of John Galsworthy - had enjoyed its first run on the new channel, BBC2. Subject of unanimously favourable reviews, it could not be picked up by old television sets, so it was decided to run it once more on BBC1, the principal British network channel. The result - a runaway hit and soaring ratings on Sunday evenings.

The series starring Eric Porter, Susan Hampshire, Nyree Dawn Porter and Kenneth More, was broadcast in 26 parts, each 50 minutes long. Sold worldwide, including to the US Public Broadcasting Service, *The Forsyte Saga* would become a recognized classic of TV costume drama.

UK TOP 10 SINGLES

1: The Good, The Bad And The Ugly
- Hugo Montenegro & Orchestra

2: With A Little Help From My Friends
- Joe Cocker

3: Eloise
- Barry Ryan

4: Those Were The Days
- Mary Hopkin

5: This Old Heart Of Mine
- The Isley Brothers

6: Only One Woman
- Marbles

7: All Along The Watchtower
- The Jimi Hendrix Experience

8: Light My Fire
- José Feliciano

9: Breakin' Down The Walls Of Heartache
- Johnny Johnson & The Bandwagon

10: Little Arrows
- Leapy Lee

NOVEMBER 6

Monkees Hit The Big Screen

The mega-successful made-for-TV group The Monkees premièred their first (and only) movie, *Head*, in New York tonight to universally indifferent reviews. Produced on a $750,000 budget, the film would prove an international box-office flop. However, due in part to the involvement of actor Jack Nicholson, it would become a cult classic.

The Monkees would be reduced to a trio in December, when Peter Tork bought his way out of his contract. By 1970, the group which had briefly been one of the world's most successful recording acts would be no more.

ARRIVALS

Born this month
18: Peter Schmeichel, Danish international football player
29: Andy Melville, Welsh international football player

DEPARTURES

Died this month:
6: Charles Munch, French conductor, aged 77
17: Mervyn Laurence Peake, UK novelist *(Titus Groan, Gormanghast,* etc), artist, aged 57
25: Upton Sinclair, US author, aged 90
28: Enid Mary Blyton, UK children's international author *(Noddy series, The Famous Five series,* etc), aged 71 *(see main story)*

NOVEMBER 29

Cream Bow Out On A High

Having announced their dissolution earlier in the year, British rock supergroup Cream – (pictured left to right) drummer Ginger Baker, guitarist Eric Clapton and bassist Jack Bruce – played their last concert together at London's Royal Albert Hall tonight.

The event was documented by film-maker Tony Palmer as *Goodbye Cream,* while a similarly titled album became their only UK No 1 album when it was issued in March 1969.

The band would reunite on a one-off basis in 1993 to celebrate their induction to the US Rock'n'Roll Hall of Fame in Cleveland, but the intervening years would witness vastly differing fortunes for the trio. Clapton would emerge from a long period of drug addiction to become one of the world's most successful recording and concert performers, while Bruce and Baker would manage to meander along separately with various groups without ever regaining their lost stardom.

NOVEMBER 6

Nixon Wins Keys To The White House

SECOND TIME PROVED lucky for Richard Milhous Nixon today when he was elected to become the new President of the US. He had failed in his previous bid in 1960, when his opponent was John F Kennedy. And, although he won by 500,000 votes this time, he only narrowly beat the combined challenge of the Democratic Party's candidate, Vice-President Hubert Humphrey, and that of the former Alabama State Governor, George Wallace, who ran as an American Independent and polled an alarming 10 million votes for his openly racist programme.

As Nixon had done in 1960, Humphrey lost the election, despite being the incumbent Vice-President – but for him the future would not see such a welcome reversal of fortune as today's success gave Nixon, despite President Johnson's last-minute announcement of a cessation of US bombing of North Vietnam (*see separate story*). President Nixon's Vice-President would be Spiro T Agnew, the former Governor of Maryland.

NOVEMBER 28

Children's Favourite Enid Blyton Dies

Enid Blyton, the British children's author responsible for the creation of favourite fictional characters such as Noddy and Big Ears, died today at the age of 71. She published her first book, a collection of poetry entitled *Child Whispers*, in 1922 and during the next 46 years went on to write over 600 more.

Although Blyton also wrote non-fictional children's educational books, there was no doubting the huge popularity of her adventure stories. Her *Famous Five* and *Secret Seven* series were the bait that hooked many a child, giving them an early love of books, and her appeal wasn't only confined to the English language, for Blyton was one of the most translated English authors.

The subject of attack by the politically correct in the late 1980s - some of her books were even banned by librarians who found them suspect - Blyton's ghost would have the last laugh as independent research proved that her simple stories were still the ones children wanted to read most.

NOVEMBER 1

British Age Of Adulthood To Be Lowered

The British Government today announced controversial new plans to lower the age of adulthood when it published the Family Law Reform Bill.

In a decade when many young teenagers became so-called 'latch key' kids, arriving home from school to houses empty of working parents, many believed that the traditional age of 21 was just too late to be receiving the symbolic key to the door.

Opponents of the change would argue that 18 was too low an age to empower most 'children' with the right to vote, to frequent establishments selling alcohol, or blithely choose who they wanted to marry.

Literary Legend John Steinbeck Dies

THE AMERICAN AUTHOR John Steinbeck (pictured), who won huge public acclaim for his novels depicting everyday life in his native California, died today on the other side of the continent, in New York. He was 66.

His first successful novel, *Tortilla Flat*, was published in 1935, gaining him immediate recognition, while his 1937 best-seller *Of Mice And Men* was only the first of a number of Steinbeck works which would be adapted for the stage and screen. It would receive an Oscar nomination for the Best Film award two years later.

In the same year, *The Grapes Of Wrath* – his most famous title of all – appeared in the bookshops. Charting the fortunes of a poor Oklahoma farming family forced to migrate to California work camps during the Depression of the 1930s, it too would form the basis of a powerful film which won John Huston a Best Director Oscar in 1940 and drew a moving, Oscar-nominated performance from actor Henry Fonda.

Another Steinbeck best-seller, *East Of Eden*, would, in 1955, provide James Dean with one of his three major film roles. In 1962 Steinbeck was awarded the Nobel Prize for Literature, one of the few occasions when most people didn't ask 'Who?', or didn't question the justice of its presentation.

Rolling Stones Join The Circus

Britain's most outrageous rock group, The Rolling Stones, today convened the most star-studded line-up yet presented to movie cameras when filming started of *The Rolling Stones' Rock'n'Roll Circus* in a Wembley, London, film studio. Those who answered the call of director Michael Lindsay-Hogg on the two-day shoot included John Lennon and Yoko Ono, Eric Clapton, Jethro Tull, The Who, Marianne Faithfull and actress Mia Farrow.

A company of clowns and acrobats completed the cast, but the *Rock'n'Roll Circus* was never to be seen by the public.

A number of sequences - an extremely frail Marianne Faithfull stumbling her way through the controversial *Sister Morphine*, Lennon and Ono wriggling in a bag, and the obvious ill-ease of Stones guitarist Brian Jones - led to the whole project being put on ice.

Some consolation was provided by the release later in the month of *Beggars Banquet*, one of the Stones' all-time finest albums. It appeared in a white cover, Decca Records having vetoed the original design of a graffiti-covered toilet wall.

Film And Stage Worlds Mourn Tallulah Bankhead

Tallulah Bankhead, the larger-than-life stage and screen star who died today at the age of 66, had all the sophistication and zest of fictional fellow-southerner Scarlett O'Hara, although she led a rather more cosmopolitan life.

Born in Alabama, the daughter of the Speaker of the House of Representatives, Bankhead embarked upon a stage career in New York in 1918, but spent the next decade working in London. Her most notable success came during the long run of Lillian Hellman's *The Little Foxes* in 1939, and in Alfred Hitchcock's propaganda film *Lifeboat*, in which passenger ship survivors were shipwrecked with the captain of the U-boat which had sunk them.

Kissinger Is New US National Security Adviser

Henry Kissinger's support and advice during the recent Presidential election campaign earned him his first US government post today when he was named as Richard Nixon's new National Security Adviser.

Although he was born in Germany, Kissinger's family was forced to flee the Nazis in the late 1930s. Since becoming Professor of Politics at Harvard University, the 45 year old had developed many influential friends in the world of politics. His objectivity and apparent neutrality in matters of party politics was shown by the fact that he had been one of the Democratic President John F Kennedy's occasional advisers in the early 1960s.

UK TOP 10 SINGLES

1: Lily The Pink
- Scaffold
2: Ain't Got No-I Got Life/ Do What You Gotta Do
- Nina Simone
3: The Good, The Bad And The Ugly
- Hugo Montenegro & Orchestra
4: One Two Three O'Leary
- Des O'Connor
5: Build Me Up Buttercup
- The Foundations
6: I'm The Urban Spaceman
- The Bonzo Dog Doo-Dah Band
7: This Old Heart Of Mine
- The Isley Brothers
8: Breakin' Down The Walls Of Heartache
- Johnny Johnson & The Bandwagon
9: Race With The Devil
- Gun
10: I'm A Tiger
- Lulu

ARRIVALS
Born this month:
2: David Batty, England international football player
31: Vanilla Ice (Robert van Winkle), US pop/rap star

DEPARTURES
Died this month:
2: John Steinbeck, US novelist, Nobel Prize winner 1962 (*see main story*)
9: Karl Barth, Swedish theologian, aged 82
12: Tallulah Bankhead, US film and stage actress (*see main story*)

DECEMBER 29

Apollo 8 Sees Dark Side Of The Moon

NASA ASTRONAUTS James Lovell, William Anders and Frank Bormann were forced to forgo the pleasures of a traditional Christmas this year because they were otherwise engaged – 250,000 miles up in space, orbiting the moon in *Apollo 8*.

The success of the latest Apollo mission meant the American space programme was still on schedule for a moon landing by the end of the decade. It also kept the US one step ahead of the Russians, whose recent lunar orbital flights had been unmanned.

The greatest tension in what had been a flawless exercise came when Apollo vanished out of communications range as Lovell, Anders and Bormann became the first men to see the dark side of the moon (Pictured - Earth as seen from the Moon). On Christmas Eve, the crew broadcast readings from the Bible, and spoke to their families.

Today's splash-down in the Pacific was, like the rest of the mission, copy-book stuff. After journeying more than half a million miles over six days and orbiting the moon 10 times, *Apollo 8* returned safely, landing less than three miles from the US recovery ship.

Cunard's Flagship Delayed

Today's planned maiden transatlantic voyage of the luxury liner, the *QE2*, was delayed because she was unready for service. Hailed as the new flagship of the Cunard line when launched on 20 September 1967, work on fitting out the £25.5 million ($50m) ship had taken longer than expected.

A similar delay would occur after a 1994 refit in Germany and Cunard would find itself the target of lawsuits from disgruntled passengers who'd paid for a cruise.

Spain Welcomes Jews, But Bans Prince

Nearly five hundred years ago the ruling monarchs of Spain, Queen Isabella and King Ferdinand, banished all Jews from the staunchly Catholic country, but not until today was that order officially revoked. The move coincided with the opening, in Madrid, of the first synagogue to be built in Spain for 600 years.

Four days later, General Franco would take the unusual step of banishing the pretender to the Spanish throne, Prince Carlos. Many Spanish royalists hoped it would not be another five hundred years before the monarchy was allowed to return.

Child Killer, 11, Gets Life

In a case which shocked and astonished the British public, 11 year old Mary Bell was today sentenced to life imprisonment for her part in the murder of two small boys. Although she did not act alone in the killings, there was universal horror at the thought of such a young child being capable of carrying out the stranglings which earned her the conviction for manslaughter.

Bell was adjudged not to have murdered the boys when doctors testified that she was mentally disturbed, but there was little prospect of successful treatment for her psychopathic disorder because of the lack of specialized psychiatric care.

YOUR 1968 HOROSCOPE

Unlike most Western horoscope systems which group astrological signs into month-long periods based on the influence of 12 constellations, the Chinese believe that those born in the same year of their calendar share common qualities, traits and weaknesses with one of 12 animals - Rat, Ox, Tiger, Rabbit, Dragon, Snake, Horse, Sheep, Monkey, Rooster, Dog or Pig.

They also allocate the general attributes of five natural elements - Earth, Fire, Metal, Water, Wood - and an overall positive or negative aspect to each sign to summarize its qualities.

If you were born between February 9, 1967 and January 29, 1968, you are a Sheep. As this book is devoted to the events of 1968, let's take a look at the sign which governs those born between January 30 that year and February 16, 1969 - The Year of The Monkey:

THE MONKEY
JANUARY 30, 1968 - FEBRUARY 16, 1969
ELEMENT: FIRE   ASPECT: (+)

Monkeys display cleverness, intelligence and quick wits and can size up any situation at a glance. With a natural cunning which gives them an ingenious and inventive mind, Monkeys learn the intricacies of social skills - how to mingle, learn and take from other people, and how to get exactly what they want from a relationship - from an early age. Their poise and self-assurance never runs out as it comes from vast resources of inborn charm which ensures them general popularity and also guarantees them fulfilment of their aims and ambitions.

Monkeys are so inventive they tend to confuse fantasy with reality so, in their scheme of things, truth and untruth often make easy bedfellows. If they are caught out, Monkeys will always somehow manage to twist the situation to their advantage to vindicate themselves and save face.

Rarely bored, Monkeys are extremely inquisitive and forever seeking the bigger and better they need to keep themselves interested and amused. Mischievous and impish, Monkeys are always trying to liven things up.

Some Monkeys can manipulate others too easily. They can read people like books and female Monkeys can play rather subtle games with those of the opposite sex, seducing them with their feminine charms.

Highly adaptable and versatile, Monkeys pick up new skills and techniques in the blink of an eye - a tremendous asset for them in all areas of life and work. With such an agile mentality, problem-solving is both their forte and their joy. They have the ability to turn their hands to anything which will bring them ultimate success and, in many cases, make their fortune.

Though their renowned adaptability takes them into many occupations, Monkeys naturally go for show business because they have a compelling need to be noticed and leave a memory of themselves behind. However, they don't really care about their reputations, so it doesn't matter to them if the impression they create is one of pleasure or shock - it's simply a case of the bigger the publicity, the happier they are.

FAMOUS MONKEYS

Sebastian Coe
British Olympic and world champion athlete, now politician

Elizabeth Taylor
Oscar-winning actress, multiple matrimonialist

Pope John Paul II

Walter Matthau
Oscar-winning character actor

Diana Ross
singing superstar, actress

Sugar Ray Leonard
former world welterweight boxing champion